DOGGIE DUTIES

David and Patricia Armentrout

www.rourkepublishing.com

www.rourkepublishing.com

Photo credits: Cover © paparazzit; Table of Contents © Liluya Kulianionak; Page 4 © Katrina Brown; Page 5 © Rhonda ODonnell; Page 6 © Toxawww; Page 7 © Jszg005, Petr Jilek; Page 8 © Andrey Bandurenko, Viorel Sima, thepiwko; Page 9 © cynoclub; Page 10 © Chris Howey; Page 11 © Chris Howey; Page 12 © Salima; Page 13 © Sandra Zuerlein; Page 14 © Joy Brown; Page 15 © John Long; Page 16 © Artem Kursin; Page 18 © iofoto, kudrashka-a; Page 19 © kudrashka-a; Page 20 © April Turner, Willeecole; Page 21 © Andrii Muzyka, Graphicphoto; Page 22 © Jszg005, Viorel Sima, Andrey Bandurenko, Chris Howey, Salima, iofoto

Editor: Jeanne Sturm

Cover and page design by Nicola Stratford, bdpublishing.com

Library of Congress Cataloging-in-Publication Data

Armentrout, David, 1962-
 Doggie duties / David and Patricia Armentrout.
    p. cm. -- (Let's talk about pets)
 Includes index.
 ISBN 978-1-61590-245-3 (hard cover)
 ISBN 978-1-61590-485-3 (soft cover)
 1. Dogs--Juvenile literature. I. Armentrout, Patricia, 1960- II. Title.
 SF426.5.A723 2011
 636.7'0887--dc22
                            2010005365

Rourke Publishing
Printed in the United States of America, North Mankato, Minnesota
010311
123010LP-A

www.rourkepublishing.com - rourke@rourkepublishing.com
Post Office Box 643328 Vero Beach, Florida 32964

TABLE OF CONTENTS

LEADER OF THE PACK

Do you know why people say a dog is man's best friend? One reason might be that dogs are **loyal**. They love their owners unconditionally. Dogs are also pack animals. Just like people, they need to be part of a group, or family.

Your dog can be a well-behaved family member if you act like the leader of the pack. That means taking control of your dog, not letting your dog control you!

Sadly, many dogs don't have a family. Their home is an **animal shelter**. When you're looking for a four-legged friend, adopting a shelter dog is a great choice.

TOUCH TEST

You can test a puppy's personality with a touch test. An accepting puppy won't mind if you pet him, pick him up, or examine his paws or mouth. A nervous pup won't like to be touched and may try to run away. A pup with an aggressive personality may growl and try to bite your hand.

DOGGIE DUTIES

Pack leaders have responsibilities. So, besides running around the house with your pooch playing tag, you also have doggie duties. Your daily duties include feeding, exercising, and yes, cleaning up after your dog.

At least once a year, you need to take your pet to the doctor, or **veterinarian**. Dogs need to see a vet for regular medical check-ups and **vaccines** that will help keep them free from disease.

A vet will examine your dog's eyes, ears, teeth, and gums.

Your veterinarian can also tell you about **spaying** and **neutering**, two methods used to help control overpopulation. Consider it your duty to help reduce the number of puppies without homes.

GROOMING TIPS

A well-groomed dog is a happier and healthier dog. Regular brushing will keep your dog's coat clean and shiny. It is also a great time to check for unwanted pests like **ticks** and fleas.

A tick

A vet can prescribe a medicine that protects your dog from fleas and ticks.

Poop Patrol

Being on poop patrol means cleaning up after your dog when on a walk or away from home. Here is a handy trick:

1. After your dog poops, put a plastic bag on your hand and wear it like a mitten.

2. Use your plastic bag mitten to pick up the poop.

3. Now wrap the bag around the poop, tie it closed, and put it in a trash container.

Most experts agree a dog needs about one fluid ounce (29.5 milliliters) of water per pound (0.45 kilograms) of body weight. However, the amount of water a dog drinks depends on its breed, size, and activity level. Just make sure your dog has fresh, clean water every day. He will drink when he is thirsty.

BOW WOW CHOW

Most dogs eat two meals a day. This helps balance **nutrient** and energy levels. How much you feed your dog depends on its age, size, and activity level.

There are lots of dog food options. Most people buy prepared food, but some dog owners choose to cook special recipes for their four-legged friends.

Large dogs need more food than small dogs. Follow food labels and feed your dog proper amounts according to his or her weight.

No matter what type of food you feed your pup, after it eats it will need to poop. Always make sure you have time to take your dog outside after it eats and before you leave the house.

DOG FOOD NO-NO'S

Be careful what you give your dog. Some people foods, like chocolate, grapes, and raisins, are **toxic** to dogs. Even small amounts can make a dog very sick.

DID YOU KNOW?

Dogs lap water by scooping it up with their tongues. Oddly, they curl their tongues under, not forward, the way we would. (Try it, if you like water in your nose!) A backwards scoop puts the water right into a dog's mouth, not all over his snout.

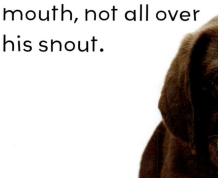

Mealtime Manners

Some dogs get excited and jump around at mealtime. Encourage good **behavior** by using simple, but strong, **commands**. Dogs are very smart. Use the same command every time. They learn quickly.

Use the command "sit" before you place the bowl of food on the floor.

Use the command "okay" to let your dog know it is time to eat.

13

PLAYTIME

Dogs need daily exercise and playtime to stay fit, trim, and happy. Most dogs love to play fetch, and the game teaches them to follow commands. After throwing a stick or toy, reward your pooch with a treat when he brings the toy back.

You can treat-train your dog to do tricks like *shake, sit, sit up,* and *roll over.* Don't forget to praise him with a gentle voice when he gets it right!

Let's all go to the dog park...

Dogs like to meet other dogs. But, they don't shake hands as people would. They say "hi" and learn about each other using their keen sense of smell. After little sniffs here and there, your dog will happily run and play with the others.

An ID tag with your phone number, address, and your dog's name is helpful in case your pup gets lost.

REMEMBER...

Bring a leash, water, and a water bowl when you take your dog away from home.

TUB-TIME TIPS

Sooner or later, your four-legged friend will need a bath. Some dogs like baths, some dogs don't. Follow these tips so bath time is easier for you and more enjoyable for your dog.

If your dog has a heavy coat of hair, brush it before the bath. This helps keep the drain from clogging with hair.

1 The best place to wash your dog is in the bathtub. Place towels on the floor around the tub, in case of splashes.

2 Wet your dog's coat, lather on the dog shampoo, and then rinse your dog completely. Be careful not to get shampoo in your dog's eyes.

3 Use a towel to dry your pooch. Keep him away from drafts until he is completely dry. Then, brush him.

PUPPY POINTERS

Puppies need special care and attention. Some practical pointers can help your puppy get started off on the right foot. (Oops, the right paw!)

Puppies lose the natural disease protection they get from their mothers' milk. Take your puppy to the veterinarian for a check-up and vaccines.

Pups need to eat several times a day. As your pup grows, you can adjust feeding to twice a day.

Good
Dog

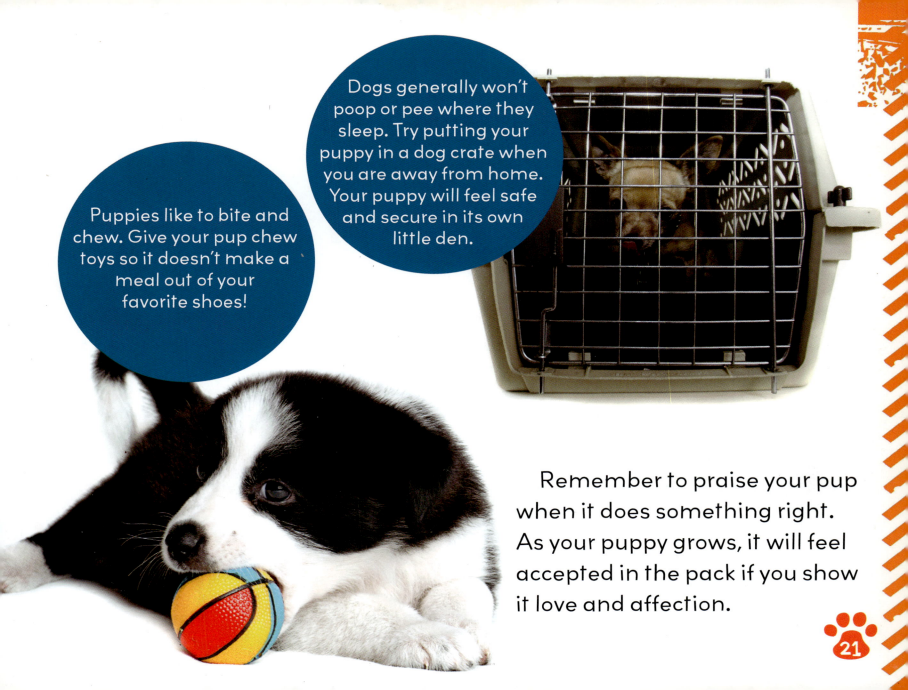

Puppies like to bite and chew. Give your pup chew toys so it doesn't make a meal out of your favorite shoes!

Dogs generally won't poop or pee where they sleep. Try putting your puppy in a dog crate when you are away from home. Your puppy will feel safe and secure in its own little den.

Remember to praise your pup when it does something right. As your puppy grows, it will feel accepted in the pack if you show it love and affection.

21

MEET SOME OF THE MODELS!

Sophie, page 7
Yorkshire Terrier

Buster, page 10
Yellow Labrador Retriever

Peanut, page 10
Chihuahua

Marley, page 12
Beagle

Scruffy, page 14
West Highland Terrier

Monty, page 18
Pomeranian

22

GLOSSARY

animal shelter (AN-uh-muhl SHEL-tur): a temporary home for lost, stray, or unwanted animals

behavior (bi-HAYV-yuhr): doing and saying things in a certain way

commands (kuh-MANDZ): orders or instructions

loyal (LOI-uhl): displaying constant belief and trust

neutering (NOO-tur-ing): surgically removing the reproductive organs in a male animal

nutrient (NOO-tree-uhnt): something needed to stay strong and healthy

spaying (SPAY-ing): surgically removing the reproductive organs in a female animal

ticks (TIKS): small insects that suck blood from under the skin of animals and people

toxic (TOK-sik): harmful or deadly

vaccines (vak-SEENZ): shots that help prevent disease

veterinarian (vet-ur-uh-NAIR-ee-un): a person trained to treat injured or sick animals

23

Index

Websites

www.animal.discovery.com/guides/dogs

www.aspca.org/dogs

www.loveyourdog.com

www.pbs.org/wgbh/woof/

About the Authors

David and Patricia Armentrout live near Cincinnati, Ohio, with their two sons and dog, Max. After adopting Max in 2001, it didn't take long before he won over the hearts of family, friends, and neighbors! The Armentrouts have also had other pets over the years, including cats, birds, guinea pigs, snakes, fish, turtles, frogs, and hermit crabs.